My Canada
SASKATCHEWAN

By Sheila Yazdani

TABLE OF CONTENTS

Saskatchewan 3

Glossary 22

Index 24

A Crabtree Seedlings Book

Crabtree Publishing
crabtreebooks.com

School-to-Home Support for Caregivers and Teachers

This book helps children grow by letting them practice reading. Here are a few guiding questions to help the reader build his or her comprehension skills. Possible answers appear in red.

Before Reading:
- What do I know about Saskatchewan?
    - *I know that Saskatchewan is a province.*
    - *I know that Saskatchewan has plains.*

- What do I want to learn about Saskatchewan?
    - *I want to learn which famous people were born in Saskatchewan.*
    - *I want to learn what the provincial flag looks like.*

During Reading:
- What have I learned so far?
    - *I have learned that Regina is the capital of Saskatchewan.*
    - *I have learned that Saskatoon is the largest city in Saskatchewan.*

- I wonder why…
    - *I wonder why the provincial flower is the western red lily.*
    - *I wonder why Saskatchewan grows so much durum wheat.*

After Reading:
- What did I learn about Saskatchewan?
    - *I have learned that you can hike in Grasslands National Park.*
    - *I have learned that the provincial animal is the white-tailed deer.*

- Read the book again and look for the glossary words.
    - *I see the word **capital** on page 6, and the word **produces** on page 11. The other glossary words are found on pages 22 and 23.*

I live in Saskatoon. I enjoy going for walks on the Meewasin Trail.

The name Saskatoon came from a **Cree** word for a type of red berry that grows in the area.

Saskatchewan is a **province** in western Canada. The **capital** is Regina.

Fun Fact: Saskatoon is the largest city in Saskatchewan.

The provincial animal is the white-tailed deer.

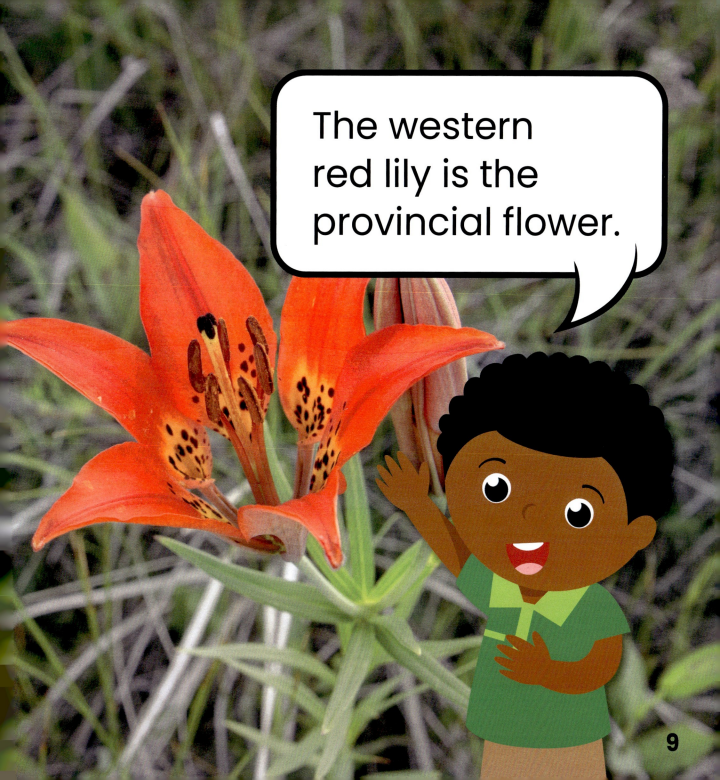

Fun Fact: Saskatchewan **produces** more than one-third of the world's durum wheat.

My provincial flag is yellow and green. Saskatchewan's **coat of arms** is in the top corner.

My family enjoys watching the Saskatoon Blades play hockey.

"I like to visit Prince Albert National Park. I have picnics with my family and swim at Waskesiu Main Beach!"

Fun Fact: Prince Albert National Park is home to more than 100 plains bison.

I enjoy learning about history at Fort Walsh National Historic Site.

I like to watch the Sergeant Major's Parade at the RCMP Heritage Centre.

Actor Leslie Neilsen was born in Saskatchewan. Hockey legend Gordie Howe was also born in Saskatchewan.

Fun Fact: Dafydd Williams, an astronaut on two space shuttle missions, was born in Saskatoon, Saskatchewan.

Doing a tour of the Tunnels of Moose Jaw is exciting!

Glossary

capital (CAP-ih-tuhl): The city or town where the government of a country, state, or province is located

coat of arms (coht uv armz): A special group of pictures, usually shown on a shield

Cree (kree): First Nations people who are among the first inhabitants of Canada

durum wheat (DUR-uhm weet): A type of grain that is often used to make pasta or bread

produces (pruh-DOOS-es): Makes or grows something for sale or use

province (PROV-ins): One of the large areas that some countries, such as Canada, are divided into

Index

durum wheat 10, 11
Neilsen, Leslie 18
Prince Albert National Park 14, 15
Regina 6
Saskatoon 4, 5, 7, 19
western red lily 9

Written by: Sheila Yazdani
Designed and Illustrated by: Bobbie Houser
Series Development: James Earley
Proofreader: Melissa Boyce
Educational Consultant: Marie Lemke M.Ed.

About the Author

Sheila Yazdani lives in Ontario near Niagara Falls with her dog Daisy. She likes to travel across Canada to learn about its history, people, and landscape. She loves to cook new dishes she learns about. Her favorite treat is Nanaimo bars.

Photographs:
Alamy: Rolf Hicker Photography: p. 16-17; NASA Image Collection: p. 19
Newscom: Derek Mortensen/ZUMAPRESS: p. 13; Jeff Goode/ZUMA Press: p. 18 right
Shutterstock: Nancy Anderson: cover, 15; Bernie Cardin: p. 3; EB Adventure Photography: p. 4-5, 22; Media Guru: p. 6, 22-23; Scott Prokop: p. 7; Michael Sean OLeary: p. 8; Lost Mountain Studio: p. 9; Lloyd Gwilliam: p. 10-11, 23; Alexander Prokopenko: p. 11; Millenius: p. 12, 22; Jason Yoder: p. 14-15; Featureflash Photo Agency: p. 18 left; Bennekom: p. 20; lynn friedman: p. 21

Crabtree Publishing

crabtreebooks.com   800-387-7650
Copyright © 2025 Crabtree Publishing
All rights reserved. No part of this publication may be reproduced, stored in a retrieval system or be transmitted in any form or by any means, electronic, mechanical, photocopying, recording, or otherwise, without the prior written permission of Crabtree Publishing. In Canada: We acknowledge the financial support of the Government of Canada through the Canada Book Fund for our publishing activities.
Printed in Canada/012024/CP20231127

Published in Canada
Crabtree Publishing
616 Welland Avenue
St. Catharines, Ontario
L2M 5V6

Published in the United States
Crabtree Publishing
347 Fifth Avenue
Suite 1402-145
New York, New York, 10016

Library and Archives Canada Cataloguing in Publication
Available at Library and Archives Canada

Library of Congress Cataloging-in-Publication Data
Available at the Library of Congress

Hardcover: 978-1-0398-3857-4
Paperback: 978-1-0398-3942-7
Ebook (pdf): 978-1-0398-4023-2
Epub: 978-1-0398-4095-9